Blossoming into Radiance

Published by
Claritza Rausch -Peralta

Disclaimer Notice:
This memoir is a recounting of my own experiences, emotions, and perspectives. There may be gaps in the narrative, details that have faded with time, or complexities that cannot be fully captured within these pages. It is not intended to be a comprehensive account of my entire life but rather a collection of selected moments and reflections that have shaped my journey.

For more information, please contact:

Claritza Rausch-Peralta

Email: Peralta.claritza@gmail.com

Phone Number : (267) 453-1426

Instagram: Claritzaperaltaa

Facebook: Claritza Rausch Peralta

Blossoming into Radiance

From: Claritza Rausch - Peralta

To:

_____

In the embracing arms of God's grace,
I found the courage to face my past, to let go
of my pain, and to embrace a future filled with
joy, forgiveness, and love.

Contents

Dedications

This dedication goes to my Heavenly Father, I humbly bow before Your infinite grace and offer this heartfelt dedication to you because amidst the trials and triumphs, You have been my guiding light, my unwavering source of strength. In times of despair, You have uplifted my spirit, reminding me of the boundless love that surrounds me, thank you so much for your forgiveness and unconditional love.

Also, to all those who have cared for me, in ways big and small, I extend my deepest gratitude. Your kindness and selflessness have touched my soul, illuminating the paths I tread. Through your acts of compassion, you have shown me the beauty of humanity, and for that, I am eternally grateful.

Grandmother, you are a beacon of love and wisdom in my life. Your gentle touch and words of encouragement have shaped me into the person I am today. In your embrace, I find solace, knowing that your love will forever guide me.

And last but not least, my dearest Liam, my precious son, you are the embodiment of joy and hope. In your laughter, I find strength, and in your innocent eyes, I see a future filled with endless possibilities. Your presence in my life has taught me the true meaning of unconditional love, and I am forever blessed to be your mother, I love you with all my heart kiddo!

Gratitude

As I reflect upon my journey, my heart overflows with gratitude for the experiences, both joyous and challenging, that have shaped me into the person I am today. I am humbled by the lessons learned, the growth achieved, and the strength discovered along the way.

From my childhood days in La Romana, Dominican Republic, to the trials and triumphs of adolescence, every chapter of my life has been a testament to resilience and determination. Through it all, I am grateful for the unwavering support of my loved ones and the unwavering love of God.

I express profound gratitude for the woman I am today, the present, as it is a gift that I cherish because each passing moment presents an opportunity to embrace the beauty of life, and to make a positive impact in the world. I am also grateful for the blessings that surround me, the love of family and friends, the abundance of opportunities, and the ability to pursue my passions.

Looking towards the future, I am filled with hope and excitement. I am grateful for the dreams that reside within me, propelling me forward. With faith as my guide, I confidently step into the unknown, knowing that every challenge is an opportunity for growth and every setback is a stepping stone towards success.

Above all, my heart is filled with gratitude for the power of forgiveness. It is through forgiveness that I have found healing, liberation, and inner peace. As I let go of grudges and embrace compassion, I open myself to a world filled with love and understanding.

In this book, I celebrate the beauty of my journey, the strength of my spirit, and the power of forgiveness and gratitude. May these words inspire others to embrace the blessings in their own lives, to rise above adversity, and to foster a spirit of forgiveness. Let us be grateful for every experience, for they have shaped us into the magnificent beings we are today.

Introduction

In the midst of life's darkest storms, there exists a ray of hope, a glimmer of light that has the power to transform even the most broken of souls. This is a story of triumph over adversity, a testament to the unfathomable love and grace of God that can breathe new life into the weary and lost.

Welcome to Blossoming into Radiance: A Memoir of How God's Love and Grace Saved My Life. Within the pages of this book, I invite you to embark on a journey - a journey that will take you through the deepest depths of despair and lead you to the soaring heights of redemption and renewal. This memoir is not about perfection or a neatly tied-up narrative; it's about my messy, complicated, and beautiful aspects of life that shape me into who I am.

My name is Claritza Rausch Peralta, and ever since I was a little girl, I've always struggled with finding my true identity and navigating the complexities of purpose, love, and relationships. It seemed like an endless journey, filled with confusion and heartbreak. However, through it all, I found solace and fulfillment in my faith in God. Growing up, I often felt lost and unsure of who I truly was, I yearned for acceptance and love, but with each rejection and disappointment, I felt as if I was floating aimlessly, searching for something that would give me a sense of direction and fulfillment.

In the darkest moments of my existence, when all seemed lost, God's love reached down and embraced me. His grace shone brightly amidst the shadows, illuminating a path towards healing and restoration. It was through His unwavering love that I found the strength to confront my past, to face my fears, and to embrace the transformation that awaited me.

You see, God is the ultimate author, and He knows exactly how to craft a beautiful narrative out of even the most tangled messes. Just like a skilled writer, He knows how to build tension, create plot twists, and ultimately bring about a satisfying resolution. He can turn our mess into a message, our pain into purpose, and our failures into opportunities for growth.

When we trust in God's plan, we can find comfort in knowing that He is working everything out for our good. It may not always make sense in the moment, but we can rest assured that every chapter of our lives is part of a bigger, grander story. And just like any great story, there will be moments of laughter, tears, love, and triumph.

Blossoming into Radiance" Is a testament to the power of faith, resilience, and the redeeming power of God's love. It is a story that carries a universal message that no matter how lost or broken we may feel, no matter how far we have strayed, there is always hope for restoration.

With an open heart and a resilient spirit, I share the trials and triumphs that have shaped me into the person I am today. From the depths of a sad childhood, through the turbulence of adolescence, to the wisdom and strength I have gained as an adult.

I have made the decision to open up in the most vulnerable way possible. It's important to me that I share my truth, raw and unfiltered, so that others may find solace and understanding in their own journeys. Through the pages of this book, I hope to inspire you to believe in the miraculous power of God's love.

May you find the courage to face your own demons and the strength to rise above them. May you find, as I did, that even the most shattered pieces of our lives can be transformed into something beautiful.

So, I invite you to turn the page and embark on this journey with me. Let us discover together the incredible healing and transformative power of God's love and grace.

May this memoir serve as a beacon of hope, guiding you towards a life of radiance and purpose.

Part One

My Childhood

Me as a little girl, in Dominican Republic

While I was living In Puerto Rico

Living in the United States

I was about 5 years old in this picture

Chapter 1

Who am I?

In the humble town of La Romana, nestled in the heart of the Dominican Republic, a radiant soul was brought into this world on a November day. That soul was me, though my true identity would remain a mystery for years to come.

I was welcomed into a world filled with love and warmth. Or so I believed. Little did I know, my journey of self-discovery was about to begin, unraveling the intricacies of my past and shaping the person I would become.

You see, from a tender age of only nine months, my biological mother entrusted me to the loving care of my grandmother. In the eyes of a child, my grandmother was my everything. My guiding light, my protector, my mother. I reveled in the joy of her presence, unaware of the secrets that lay hidden beneath the surface.

It wasn't until the tender age of seven that the truth was unveiled, shattering the illusion I had held onto for so long. My grandmother, the woman I had adored and revered, was not my biological mother. The revelation sent shockwaves through my young heart, leaving me with so many emotions and questions.

Who am I, really? Where do I come from? These questions danced in my mind, fueling a relentless curiosity within me. And so, my journey of self-discovery began, a quest to find the missing pieces of my identity.

I remember it like it was yesterday, the day my innocent world was shattered into a million pieces.

"Mama Luisa" was everything to me, she still is. Her love was like an unstoppable force, enveloping me in its comforting embrace. She was my guiding light, my rock, and my confidante. I cherished our moments together, whether it was watching a " Novela" together, walking to church with my "Madrina" Eroina, or making me breakfast and taking me to school "La escuelita"

But one day, my neighbor who is like family to us sat with me with a pained expression on her face and told me;

"Mama Luisa isn't your real mother"

I struggled to comprehend the reality that had been concealed from me for so long. Questions swirled in my mind, demanding answers that seemed just out of reach.

Who was my real mother? Why had this secret been kept from me? And most importantly, why did it hurt so much?

Before finding out that my grandmother wasn't actually my mother, I had a wonderfully happy childhood as a little girl. Growing up on my block, known as "Los Multis Familiares," I was quite the popular kid. My best friend, who was like a sister was Dorys, and I had friends all around and always found myself visiting neighbors houses. In fact, I even lived with a couple of them from time to time, as my grandmother had a Visa and needed to travel back and forth between Puerto Rico and the Dominican Republic.

Those were truly some of the best times of my life. The warmth and love I felt from my neighbors was incredible. They treated me like their own, and I felt like I had an extended family right there on the block. We would play games, share meals, and make unforgettable memories together.

My grandmother, who I believed to be my mother at the time always made sure I felt loved and cared for. Her frequent travels never diminished the bond we shared, as she would always return with stories and gifts that made me feel special and cherished.

Discovering the truth about my biological mother was a life altering moment. It was painful and confusing, to say the least, it was quite a shock to me. It was like someone had rearranged all the puzzle pieces of my identity, and suddenly, I had to figure out where I fit in.

I questioned everything I had known about myself, my family, and my place in the world.

But it didn't change the fact that my grandmother taught me the power of love, resilience, and unbreakable bonds.

From the moment I entered her life, "Mama Luisa" embraced me with open arms, showering me with warmth and affection. She saw beyond the superficial and recognized the essence of my being. She has dedicated her life to supporting and uplifting me, always putting my needs before her own.

Even when we are physically apart, I could feel her presence in my heart, guiding me towards the path of righteousness.

She will always hold a special place in my heart, as the woman who loved me unconditionally and shaped the person I am today.

But, that did not change the fact that, as a kid, I found myself grappling with a myriad of emotions. I couldn't comprehend how something so fundamental, something that defined my very existence, had been hidden from me for so long.

Chapter 2

A Life Changing Surprise

"Mama Luisa" surprised me with the most incredible news that we are traveling to Puerto Rico.

A surge of pure joy washed over me as I realized the immense significance of this opportunity of traveling with my grandmother to a place so different from my homeland, the Dominican Republic. It was my very first time on an airplane, and I was filled with excitement and butterflies in my stomach. I was about to embark on a journey to Puerto Rico, and I couldn't wait to explore this beautiful island with my grandmother by my side. I knew deep within my soul that this journey would be nothing short of transformative, and it was the moment we set foot on the island, an inexplicable connection formed.

Puerto Rico welcomed me with open arms. On that very first day, I found myself surrounded by Aunts and Uncles. In their presence, I felt a deep sense of belonging, a profound connection to a part of me that had been waiting to be discovered. I was truly happy. Later my Aunt arrived in her car to pick me up, beaming with excitement. She had planned a special outing for us, and I couldn't wait to see where she was taking me. As we drove along the vibrant streets of Puerto Rico, she told me all about her restaurant in Piñones.

The moment we stepped inside the restaurant, I was greeted by the warm aroma of delicious Puerto Rican cuisine. The walls were adorned with vibrant artwork, depicting the rich history and culture of the island. She insisted that I try her famous mofongo, a dish made with mashed plantains and a variety of savory fillings. It was a true culinary masterpiece, bursting with flavors that danced on my taste buds. As I ate she shared stories of her journey in the restaurant industry, she told me she also had a restaurant at the beach and that she would take me on the weekends.

I was truly happy to be in Puerto Rico.

The vibrant colors, the warm tropical breeze, and the welcoming smiles of the locals instantly made me feel at home. Every corner I turned, there was something new to discover and explore. I left Piñones with a heart full of gratitude and a newfound appreciation for the vibrant culture and culinary delights of Puerto Rico.

That night as I arrived at my house, little did I know that destiny had something in store for me, when the house phone rang, and as I picked it up, a familiar voice filled my ears. It was my uncle, calling me to tell me to be ready tomorrow morning because he was taking me to meet someone special.

Who could this mysterious special someone be?
I imagined all the possibilities, feeling a sense of wonder and excitement flood my being. Little did I know that this encounter would change the course of my life forever.

As we arrived, I found my eyes searching for that special someone that my uncle said he wanted me to meet. As I looked around, there was a woman, that came outside her house to say hi to my uncle. She asked him who the little girl was, and my uncle asked me if I knew who she was.

That day I met my biological mother.

The day I met my mom is a memory that will forever be etched in my heart. It was a mix of emotions, fear, nervousness, uncertainty. I didn't know how to react or what to say.

Should I have hugged tightly, letting all the emotions pour out? Or should I have burst into tears, overwhelmed with a flood of emotions that had been building up for years? Maybe I should have whispered to my uncle, asking if we could leave, feeling too overwhelmed to face this moment.

But amidst all these conflicting thoughts, I knew deep down that this was a chance I couldn't let slip away.

Meeting my biological mother was
a moment that held the potential to bring closure, understanding, and a sense of identity.

I was shocked. As I approached her, my heart was pounding in my chest. It was clear she was shocked too and had been waiting for this moment.

I took a deep breath, summoning all the courage I had within me and reached out to hug her.

Tears streamed down my face. I didn't know what to say.

In that moment, I realized that meeting my biological mother wasn't just about me. It was about embracing the past, no matter how complicated or painful it may have been.

As I walked into her house, I noticed beers, cigarettes, and very loud music. I was confused. I felt strange.

I met my other sisters and we spent the rest of the day talking, and getting to know each other.

And as I looked at my mom my questions only multiplied.

Why did she choose to walk away? What were her reasons? Why didn't I have the chance to speak to her in the Dominican Republic? And now that I'm at her house why is there so much alcohol and cigarettes around the house? Did they play a role in her decision to leave? Were they a coping mechanism? Or were they simply a reflection of her struggles and hardships?

I approached the topic with an open heart and a desire to understand. I knew that blaming her would not bring me the closure I sought. Instead, I yearned for a connection, an opportunity to have a conversation and find some closure, but still I felt like I did not belong here.

You see, meeting your biological mother can be a big deal for many people. It's a moment that's often filled with anticipation, curiosity, and maybe even some anxiety. But for me, it was different. I just didn't feel that same excitement or desire to meet her or anyone.

Instead, my heart longed for my grandmother. She was the one who nurtured me, who taught me life lessons, and who always made me feel safe and comfortable.

I simply felt content with the family I already had.

I called up my uncle, and asked him to pick me up.
As I got into the car, I couldn't help but feel a sense of relief. The weight of the momentous occasion was lifted off my shoulders, and I was finally able to process everything that had just happened.

As we drove towards my grandmother's house, a wave of emotions began to wash over me. Thoughts of my childhood, the countless memories, and the unconditional love I received from her flooded my mind. I couldn't help but feel an overwhelming sense of gratitude for having her in my life.

When we arrived at the house, I stepped out of the car and saw her waiting on the porch. The sight of her warm smile instantly brought tears to my eyes. Without hesitation, I rushed towards her and hugged her tightly, unable to contain the flood of emotions any longer.

At that moment, I realized that it didn't matter what had transpired or what had brought me to this point in my life. My grandmother was my true mother, the one who had always been there, loving and supporting me unconditionally and it was in that moment that I knew, without a doubt, that my grandmother's love would always be the most precious gift in my life.

But little did I know that my life was about to take an unexpected turn once again.

A couple months later, my family sat me down and gently broke the news. That I would be moving to Philadelphia to live with my Aunt and that I would like it there, because she had a daughter my age, and I would love the snow.

I couldn't comprehend the magnitude of this decision. Questions raced through my mind as usual, and a mixture of excitement and apprehension filled my heart, but as an eight year old kid of course I was excited to see the snow.

Chapter 3

Pennypack Street

When I first arrived in the United States, I remember feeling a chill run through my body as I stepped off the airplane. Coming from Puerto Rico, a warmer climate, I wasn't quite prepared for the cold weather that greeted me. But little did I know that the warmth of my aunt's love and the excitement of seeing her and her family waiting for me at the airport would quickly melt away any lingering chill.

As I made my way through the airport, my heart raced with anticipation. It had been years since I had seen my Aunt, and the thought of being reunited with her filled me with joy.
I couldn't help but smile as I spotted her familiar face in the crowd. She looked just as I remembered her, white skin and beautiful. "Hola Clari" She said and hug me.

As we made our way to the car, my Aunt's family greeted me with open arms and wide smiles. They were just as eager to meet me as I was to see them. I met her husband, his daughter, her son, and I saw Melissa again. I remembered her because I met her in the Dominican Republic, when she onced went with her mom.

Finally, after what seemed like an eternity, I had arrived at Pennypack Street. As I stepped out of the car and took in my surroundings, I couldn't help but feel a sense of excitement and anticipation. This was going to be my new home, and I couldn't wait to explore everything it had to offer. I met my cousins, Andia, Deida, and Willy that also lived there.

My new home in Pennypack was quite different from the house I lived in Puerto Rico, but in a good way.
The house was much more spacious and it had multiple rooms allowing us to have more privacy and personal space. It felt wonderful to have so much room to move around.

Me and my cousin Melissa, became sisters and went everywhere together. We dressed up for Halloween, hung out with friends around the block, got our nails done, and we did literally everything together.

Soon Pennypack Street quickly became more than just an address to me; it became a place where I felt a sense of belonging. The friendly neighbors welcomed me with open arms, and the tight-knit community made it easy to forge new friendships. From block parties to impromptu barbecue gatherings, there was always something happening on Pennypack Street.

One of the highlights of living on Pennypack Street was attending the nearby Thomas Holmes School.

My first year at Thomas Holme School, where do I even begin?

It was quite a rollercoaster ride. I started in second grade, and coming all the way from Puerto Rico, I found myself in a whole new world, surrounded by a language I barely understood and without any friends by my side. It was tough, to say the least.

Not knowing English made everything twice as challenging. Simple tasks like ordering lunch or asking for directions became massive hurdles for me. I often found myself feeling lost and frustrated, unable to fully express myself or understand what others were saying.

But you know what? Despite the initial difficulties, I never gave up. I was determined to make the most out of my time at Thomas Holme School, no matter what, and little by little, things started to change for the better.

I remember my first teacher, Mrs. Brown, she was incredibly patient and understanding. She made sure to break things down for me, using visuals and gestures to help me grasp the language. I must admit, it was a bit embarrassing at times, but Mrs. Brown's kindness and encouragement kept me going. Unfortunately, she died that year, may she rest in peace.

Due to my language barrier, I had to repeat second grade. I then had Mrs. Norton, the teacher I considered the best teacher ever, and that's when my English started picking up.

By the time I got to third grade, something amazing happened. I finally knew English!

It was such a big milestone for me, and I couldn't wait to start communicating with my classmates and making new friends.

Little did I know that this would be the beginning of a lifelong friendship.

One of the first people I connected with was a girl named, Nina. Nina and I from the moment we met, it was like we had known each other forever. We quickly became inseparable, and our bond grew stronger with each passing day.

As kids we shared secrets, laughed together, and supported one another through both good times and bad.

We also found ourselves becoming quite popular at school. It was such a surreal experience for two young kids like us, but we embraced! It was incredible to witness the power of friendship and how it could bridge gaps between different cultures, languages, and backgrounds. Our friendship became a catalyst for unity and acceptance within our school.

Nina and I shared countless adventures together, from sleeping at each other's house, buying snacks at Wawa before school, going out with her family and so much more. We laughed, we cried, and we created memories that would last a lifetime.

Third grade was hands down one of the best school years of my life. Not only did I have fantastic teachers and make amazing friends, but my family also moved to a new house on Outlook which made everything even more exciting.

The house on Outlook was a true gem!
It was so much bigger and nicer than the one on Pennypack.
From the moment you step through the front door, you'll be amazed by the spaciousness and beauty of this place.
Melissa and I shared a room, and we would always had friends over. The backyard was the highlight of this house, we had a pool and a beautiful golf course view.

I was also happy with the fact that my new house was much closer to school, just a few blocks away. I remember how thrilled I was when I found out that school was just a couple blocks away. It was such a wonderful feeling to leave my house in the morning and embark on a short, leisurely stroll to school.

During those walks to school, I would often stop by Nina's house, She lived just a few houses down from mine, and our friendship blossomed even more during that school year.

We would giggle and chat about our plans for the day, eagerly anticipating the adventures that awaited us at school.

Chapter 4

Relationships and Rejections

Growing up, I always felt like an outsider, craving acceptance and love from those around me. It seemed that no matter how hard I tried, I was always met with rejection. The rejection I felt from the feeling that I didn't grow up with my parents left a lasting impact on my self-esteem and confidence. I began to build walls around my heart, fearing that if I let anyone in, they would eventually hurt me too. This feeling of being unwanted and unloved followed me throughout my childhood and into my adolescent years, until I encountered the transformative power of God's love and grace. Lets continue reading this chapter.

In fourth grade, Nina and I were still the best of friends. We would always find time to play double Dutch at recess and sit together at the same table for lunch. Our friendship extended beyond school too, as we would often hang out on the weekends. Those were the days filled with laughter, fun, and countless memories. Whether we were exploring the neighborhood, having sleepovers, or going on adventures, Nina and I were inseparable. I also remember those elementary school crushes, It was such a fun and innocent time, full of new feelings and exciting discoveries. One person who made my heart flutter was a kid that for some reason Nina and I thought he was so cute. It's funny to think back on those days and how we would giggle and whisper about him during recess or lunchtime.

He was funny, and handsome. I remember feeling butterflies in my stomach whenever he was around. It was a mix of excitement and nervousness, not knowing what to say or how to act. Those were the moments that made my elementary school so memorable.

But for some reason, I couldn't tell him that I liked him or shake the feeling that he didn't really like me. I know it may sound silly to dwell on such things from our childhood, but it was during that time that I started to recognize the sting of rejection and insecurities.
As I grew I had a tendency to compare and question myself or my relationships. I often felt a sense of abandonment, and I carried that emotional baggage with me as I grew older.

It's funny how our childhood experiences can shape the way we perceive and approach relationships later in life. For me, it was difficult to fully trust and open up to someone, fearing that they too would leave me just like my mother did. This led to a constant need for reassurance and the fear of rejection. However, the feeling of insecurity and rejection was not solely tied to my mother's absence. It was further compounded by the experiences I had while living with my Aunt. Although she took me in and provided for my basic needs, there was an undeniable emotional void in our relationship.

Now that I'm older, I find myself reflecting on my childhood and how much I wish I was raised by both my mom and dad. The challenges and difficulties I faced growing up have made me acutely aware of the impact that a stable and loving home environment can have on a child's well-being. Growing up without both parents present in my life was undoubtedly tough. I can't help but wonder how different things could have been if I had experienced the love and support of both my mom and dad.

Throughout my life, I've faced my fair share of relationship issues, and it hasn't always been easy. I've struggled with feeling of abandonment, low self-esteem, and the pain of being humiliated or neglected.

Sometimes, we find ourselves in situations where we feel like we're constantly being let down or left behind. These feelings o abandonment can trigger deep-seated insecurities and make it difficult to trust others. It's hard not to question our own worth when we're constantly questioning why someone would choose to walk away from us.

Humiliation can also play a significant role in how we perceive ourselves in relationships. When we're repeatedly subjected to embarrassment or ridicule, it's natural to start doubting our own value. We may start to believe that we're not deserving of love and affection, and this can have a profound impact on our ability to form healthy connections with others.

Neglect, whether intentional or unintentional, can be incredibly damaging to our sense of self-worth. When we feel ignored or overlooked, it can lead to feelings of insignificance and loneliness. We may start to question why we're not important enough to receive the attention and care we desire.

But here's what I have learned today.

We are not defined by our past experiences or the challenges we've faced. We have the power to heal and grow from these difficult moments.

Besides the fact, in fourth grade, everything began to fall into place and, my world started making sense.

I also got adopted.

Despite the relationship I had with my adopted mother as a child. I can't help but feel blessed and overwhelmed with gratitude when I think about my adopted dad. He has been an incredible presence in my life, someone who has loved and supported me unconditionally.

At that time I finally felt a second chance at happiness and a sense of belonging. I found myself surrounded by family, amazing friends, and I even became quite popular in school.

I remember the feeling of walking into the classroom each morning, greeted by warm smiles and friendly hellos. My friends in fourth grade were truly exceptional. They were the kind of friends who always had your back, who made you feel accepted and loved for exactly who you were. Fourth grade brought with it a sense of belonging and purpose. I discovered my strengths and interests, and I was encouraged to pursue them wholeheartedly. Whether it was through participating in school activities, showcasing my creativity, or excelling academically, I had a newfound sense of purpose and direction.

But, of course, that didnt last so long, months later I received some unexpected news from my Aunt that turned my world upside down. I was told that I had to go back to my country, the Dominican Republic.

I never fully understood why my Aunt made the decision to take me back to the Dominican Republic.
From my understanding, it was because I was living in the United States illegally, but honestly I felt that there was more.

I remember that moment vividly from my childhood when she broke the news to me that I would be returning the Dominican Republic. As a 10-year-old, I must admit, I was filled with a surge of anger that I had never experienced before. I had grown accustomed to the life I had built here. The thought of leaving behind my friends, school, and everything familiar to me was just too much to bear. I couldn't understand why I had to leave everything behind and start anew. I felt like a small boat being tossed in a stormy sea, unable to control my own destiny. The anger welled up inside me, fueling feelings of frustration and confusion.

Now, as an adult, I reflect on that time with a different perspective. Firstly, I want to emphasize that I no longer hold no resentment towards my Aunt and for her decisions.
I bless and forgive her.
I recognize that at that time she made decisions out of concern for the well- being of her family.

I was too young to fully grasp the complexities of immigration laws and the challenges they might have faced or to know exactly what was going on. In the end, what matters most is how we choose to move forward from our past experiences.

But at that time, I simply knew that I was leaving behind friends, school, and the only home I now knew.

The most emotional moments of my life was when I had to break the news to my friends and classmates that I was returning to my country right before entering middle school. It was definitely a tearful experience for all of us, as I went on explaining the reasons for my departure, tears began to well up in my eyes. I tried my best to hold them back, but the emotions were overwhelming. I looked around and noticed that my friends and classmates were emotional too. It was hard to see them upset, knowing that our time together was coming to an end.

This part of my life was also confusing and emotional for me, as I grappled with the loss of familiarity and the uncertainty of what awaited me in the Dominican Republic.

I have to admit, I was pretty scared and nervous.

I just kept thinking to myself, would I remember enough Spanish to communicate with everyone? Would they accept me as one of their own, even though I had spent most of my life in a different country?

I wasn't sure what to expect.

Part Two

Embracing God's Love to Overcome Life's Trials

Living in the Dominican Republic

My High School years

When I was pregnant with my son Liar

Back in the United States

My graduation from
University Of Phoenix.

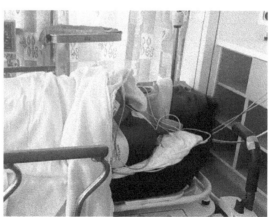

My car accident in which I almost lost
my life.

Chapter 5

La Romana

Returning back to the Dominican Republic after living in the United States was one of the saddest moments of my life. It was a whirlwind of emotions, leaving behind the place I had come to call home, the friends I had made, and the language I had learned.

I remember stepping off the plane, feeling a mix of excitement and anxiety. I knew that returning to my home country meant reuniting with my family and familiar surroundings, but it also meant facing the challenges of readjusting to a life I had left behind years ago.

One of the biggest obstacles I faced was the language barrier. In the United States, I had become fluent in English and had grown accustomed to communicating effortlessly with those around me. But upon returning to the Dominican Republic, I realized that my Spanish had become rusty. It was frustrating to stumble over my words and struggle to express myself as I had once done so fluently. Another source of sadness was leaving behind the friends I had made in the United States. We had shared countless memories and adventures, and it was heartbreaking to say goodbye to each and every one of them. I knew that I would miss their laughter, their support, and their companionship. It felt like a piece of my heart was being left behind.

This also meant readjusting to a different lifestyle. The pace of life was slower, and the cultural differences were more pronounced. It took time to adapt and find my place in this new environment. I missed the convenience and efficiency of life in the United States, and it was hard to let go of the comfort and familiarity I had grown accustomed to.

One of the greatest factors that helped me adjust to my new life was the presence of my grandmother, of course "Mama Luisa was with me. Being with her again brought a sense of comfort and familiarity that made the transition much smoother. Having her by my side made me feel safe and reassured that everything would be alright.

Not only did she provide emotional support, but she also helped me navigate the practical aspects of my new life. From teaching me how to navigate the neighborhood again, to introducing me to new friends, she made sure I had all the tools I needed to thrive in this new environment.

I eventually found solace in reconnecting with my family and familiar faces.

As time went on, I grew more and more accustomed to my new life. The initial feelings of uncertainty and unease slowly gave way to a sense of belonging and familiarity. And throughout this entire process, my grandmother remained my constant source of love and support.

As the saying goes, all good things must come to an end. The time came when my grandmother had to return to her home in Puerto Rico. It was a bittersweet farewell, filled with tears and promises to stay in touch. Little did I know that this would mark the beginning of a nightmare that I never could have anticipated.

I found myself once again living from one house to another, never having a place to call home. The sense of stability that I had briefly experienced with my grandmother was now replaced by uncertainty and constant change.

Each move brought a new set of challenges and adjustments. I had to adapt to different environments, different routines, and different faces. It was exhausting, both physically and emotionally. The constant uprooting left me feeling lost, as if I were floating aimlessly in a sea of uncertainty.

During my time living in the Dominican Republic, I had the experience of moving around approximately ten different times or more if i'm not mistaken.

I began to notice a subtle shift in my mood. It was during this period that I believe my depression started to take hold. The constant upheaval and lack of stability took a toll on my mental well-being. I had to adjust to new routines, familiarize myself with unfamiliar surroundings, and say goodbye to the sense of familiarity and comfort that a stable home provides. It left me feeling disoriented and disconnected.

The first place I lived was with my uncle. Tío Puro and his girlfriend, Margo. It wasn't such a bad experience, and today I am grateful because years later my dear uncle whom I loved so much passed away. But while I lived with them, Margo was kind and understanding and she made me feel welcome in her home.
However, circumstances changed and I had to move again. Then I found myself living with the neighbor next door. It was a different dynamic, but I appreciated her willingness to give me a place to stay during that time.

Afterwards, I ended up living with my best friend Dorys' family. Since I was a child, they have always cared for me and loved me like another daughter. They opened their doors without hesitation, treating myself as one of them. It was comforting to have her love and support, and I will always be grateful for them. What made her family so special to me was her unconditional love and acceptance. They never made me feel like a stranger living with them, but instead accepted me as part of their family.

Then I found myself living with my aunt, which was another story.
I also got to stay with relatives on my biological mother's side. What is life like right?

And well, that's how I spent it, living from one house to another. This became a regular occurrence and every time I had to pack my belongings I felt like I was ripping out a part of my soul. It was difficult to establish any sense of belonging or stability in my life. I longed for a place I could call home, a place where I could feel safe, loved and protected.

You might be wondering why I haven't mentioned my dad in this book until now.

Well, the truth is, I didn't grow up with my dad by my side, but that doesn't mean I don't love him. I am grateful to him for giving birth to me and for the financial support he provided when I needed it. However, when it comes to an emotional connection, it's something that I've never really felt with him until I grew older.

Growing up, my dad and I had a distant relationship. Remember I was raised by my grandmother, went to Puerto Rico, which is where he lives, but then left for the United States, and then I was in the Dominican Republic again.

We didn't spend much time together, and our conversations were often limited to superficial topics, but I was ok with that I am sure he had his own personal issues going own too.

But, we actually got closer when I moved with his then wife.

Chapter 6

Lost In the Darkness

I was so depressed that at times I wished I would never open my eyes again.

My life truly was like a rollercoaster ride, filled with twists and turns that I never anticipated. From when I discovered that my grandmother, the woman I had always believed to be my mother, was not my biological parent.

Then having to come back to my country the Dominican Republic after feeling like I was finally home in the U.S and as I tried to come to terms with this revelation,
to make matters worse, I found myself living from house to house, never having a place I could truly call home.

This constant state of instability left me physically and emotionally exhausted. Each move felt like another blow to my already fragile state of mind.The combination of feeling abandoned, the struggle to adapt to a new life, and the continuous lack of stability took a toll on my mental health.

I sank deeper into the darkness of depression, losing hope and motivation along the way.

Living with my dad's new girlfriend in the begining was a nightmare.

It seemed like we were from different worlds, and it felt like she just didn't understand me. I'm sure the feeling was mutual.

I couldn't help but feel that she saw me as some sort of threat, someone who was going to take my dad away from her or something...

Oh, I forgot to mention that my dad dated Margo's sister, which I also lived with before my dad met her, I got along with them very well, I feel like this made things even more difficult for us to connect and find common ground.

I found myself talking more with my dad though.

It's like a whole new level of connection was unlocked between us. And in those conversations, I mustered up the courage to share with him that I haven't been doing okay.

But, how do I tell a stranger at that time, a person that I barely knew, my step mother, that I was going through depression?

I felt a whirlwind of mixed feelings, ranging from loneliness to sadness, anxiety to depression, and even a sense of abandonment. Loneliness crept in as I struggled to connect with my stepmother on a deeper level.

Months passed and we were still getting to know each other, and it took time for us to build a bond. There were times when I felt like a stranger in my own home, longing for the familiarity of my previous family dynamic.

I didn't know what to feel anymore. It was a whirlwind of emotions that constantly left me questioning my own thoughts and feelings. At times I felt grateful that I at least had a roof over my head and a bed to sleep in, but then there were times when felt incredibly alone. It was during those moments that I felt a deep sense of loss and longing.

Anxiety also became a constant companion during this time.

The fear of not being accepted or loved by my stepmother weighed heavily on my mind. I worried if I would fit into her life if she would understand me, and if we would ever really connec It was a constant battle of doubts and worries.

Some days it felt like a dark cloud was hanging over me, making it difficult to find joy or motivation.
I struggled to find a sense of purpose and had to work hard to maintain a positive mindset.

Feeling a sense of abandonment was perhaps one of the most difficult emotions to overcome.

So, picture this, I suddenly found myself living with my dad's girlfriend whom I barely knew.

It was definitely an interesting situation, to say the least.

What made it even more peculiar was the fact that she was actually my teacher. Yep, you heard that right. The woman I now shared a living space with was my very own teacher.

and did I mention she was a Christian?

When I first moved in with my stepmother, I didn't know much about God. Growing up, my grandmother was Catholic, and we would occasionally go to church on Sundays, but my understanding of God was fairly shallow.

As time went by, I began to observe her daily habits. She would spend time in prayer and I would find her reading her Bible at times. For some reason I couldn't help but be drawn to that.

One evening, I had the courage to ask her about her faith. I wanted to understand her relationship with God, christianity in general. She patiently explained to me the basics of Christianity and shared how her faith had transformed her life.

It was a conversation that planted a seed of curiosity in my heart.

Chapter 7

A Divine Encounter

In the midst of my depression, I found myself yearning to know more about God. I was desperate for answers, for hope, and for a way out of the darkness that seemed to consume me. One day, I mustered up the courage to pray and asked Him to please help me, found myself on my knees, pouring out my heart and soul to God, begging for help. It was a moment of vulnerability and honesty, as I questioned whether God truly existed. I pleaded with sincerity, asking for a sign, a glimmer of hope that could restore my faith.

I cried out, "If you are real, please, please help me."

It was a simple prayer, filled with sincerity and a genuine desire to find solace in His presence. I didn't know what to expect, but held onto a glimmer of faith that maybe, just maybe, God would hear my plea.

As the nights arrived, so did my tears, cascading down my cheeks in an unending stream. I remember like it was yesterday, it was a Saturday night, that night I cried myself to sleep of desperation.

That Sunday morning, my stepmother approached me with an invitation that would forever change my life. She invited me to join her for a service at her church. Intrigued and open-minded, I accepted her invitation, unaware of the profound encounter with God that awaited me.

When she invited me to attend church with her, I felt a mix of nervousness and curiosity bubbling within me. As someone who had never stepped foot inside a Christian church before, I wasn't sure what to expect. But deep down, I knew that this was an opportunity for growth and new experiences, so I decided to embrace it with an open heart.

Walking into the church, I was immediately struck by the warm and welcoming atmosphere. The sense of community and unity within the congregation was palpable, and I instantly felt at ease. Listening to the sermon, I found myself captivated by the preacher's words of wisdom and grace. Each sentence resonated deeply within me, stirring my soul in ways I had never experienced before. It was as if the preacher was speaking directly to me, addressing the doubts and fears that had been lingering in my mind. Midway through his sermon, he paused and said, "There is someone here today who needs to hear this. Psalm 27:10 says, 'Though your father and mother forsake you, the Lord will receive you"

As he stood before the congregation, delivering his sermon with passion and conviction, I couldn't help but notice his searching gaze. It was as if his eyes were drawn towards me, seeking a connection, a shared understanding that went beyond the mere words he spoke.

When he called me out by my name, I was shocked and I couldn't help but feel a sense of anticipation and curiosity. Little did I know that this encounter would touch my heart in ways I could never have imagined.

As he began to pray for me, it was as if he had a divine insight into my life. He spoke of everything I had been through since I was a little girl, my mother leaving me, my emptiness and loneliness, recounting moments and struggles that I had never shared with anyone. It was both shocking and comforting to realize that God was aware of every detail of my journey.

As his words resonated through the sanctuary, I felt a profound sense of peace wash over me. The preacher spoke with unwavering conviction, assuring me that God had a unique purpose for my life. It was as if the heavens themselves had opened up, revealing a path that was destined solely for me.

He also revealed a glimpse of the future that awaited me. He whispered words of assurance, proclaiming that I would soon return to the United States. It was a revelation that filled my heart with hope and anticipation, for I longed to be reunited with the land that had shaped me into who I am.

But the preacher's prophetic message did not end there. He spoke of blessings that would surpass my wildest dreams, blessings that would touch not only my life but also those around me. It was an awe-inspiring proclamation that ignited a fire within me, a fire to live a life of purpose and make a difference in this world.

Tears welled up in my eyes as I felt a presence, which then found out it was the presence of the Holy Spirit enveloping me. It was an overwhelming sensation, a deep connection with a higher power that I had yearned for all my life. In that moment, I knew that God was reaching out to me, offering His love, understanding, and guidance.

The preacher's words resonated deeply within my soul. It was as God was speaking directly to me, reminding me that I was not alone in my struggles. The weight of the burdens I had carried for so long began to lift, replaced by a sense of peace and reassurance.

In that sacred moment, I realized that God had been with me every step of the way, even during the darkest times. He had seen me through the challenges, the heartbreaks, and the moments of doubt. It was a profound revelation that filled me with gratitude and a renewed sense of purpose.

While he was praying for me a surge of emotions washed over, and I felt an indescribable connection to something greater than myself. It was as if the universe aligned, guiding me towards a path of enlightenment and redemption.
In that powerful prayer, I accepted Jesus into my heart.

With every word spoken, my heart opened wider, embracing the love and grace that Jesus offered. I felt a profound sense of liberation, as though the weight of the world had been lifted off my shoulders.

From that day forward, my faith was strengthened, this encounter with God that transformed my life forever. It was a moment of divine intervention, a meeting with the Almighty that provided me with everything I needed to move forward and embark on a journey of forgiveness and self-transformation.

In that encounter, I realized that forgiveness was not only a choice but also a powerful tool for healing and growth. God showed me that holding onto anger and resentment was like carrying a burden that weighed me down, trapping me in a cycle of pain. He gently whispered to my heart, urging me to release the shackles of bitterness and extend forgiveness to those who had wronged me. In that moment, I understood that forgiveness is not about condoning the actions of others or forgetting the pain they caused. It is about liberating ourselves from the chains of the past, releasing the negative energy that binds us, and making room for love and joy to fill our hearts once more. God's presence filled me with a renewed sense of purpose and strength. He reminded me that I am not defined by my past mistakes or the hurtful actions of others. He assured me that I have the power to turn my life around, to create a future filled with love, compassion, and forgiveness.

That encounter with God continues to be a significant turning point in my life. It serves as a constant reminder of His unwavering love and presence. Whenever I face difficulties, I draw strength from that moment, knowing that I am not alone. I am forever grateful for the preacher's prayer and the divine touch I experienced, for it has shaped my faith and brought me closer to God.
As I'm writting and remembering this moment, I'm in tears.

Chapter 8

Navigating storms with Resilience

My life took a complete turn for the better, it's truly amazing how my perspective on life shifted and I was now seeing things in a whole new light.

I used to go through life feeling lost and disconnected. Constantly searching for meaning and purpose, but the moment I opened my heart to God, everything changed.

I felt an overwhelming sense of peace and comfort. It was as if a weight had been lifted off my shoulders, and I no longer felt alone in this world. I knew that God was with me, guiding me through every step of my journey.

With this newfound faith, I started seeing the beauty in the simplest of things. I began to appreciate the little moments that I used to overlook. It was like experiencing life for the first time, with a heart full of gratitude.

My relationship with my stepmother improve significantly, I am forever grateful to my stepmother for leading me to God and showing me the path towards spiritual enlightenment.

Moreover, my relationships with others also flourished. I started to see people not just as individuals, but as children of God, deserving of love, kindness, and forgiveness.

In the realm of forgiveness, miracles happen. They shape our hearts, heal our wounds, and free our spirits.

I forgave my mom for the pain she caused me, for the absence that left an indelible mark on my soul. I understood that she, too, had her battles, her own struggles to face. Through forgiveness, I released the burden of anger and resentment, and in return, I found a newfound sense of peace.

I forgave my aunt and the rest of my family, for the misunderstandings and conflicts that had haunted our relationships. I saw that holding grudges only perpetuated the cycle of pain. So, I chose to break free from that cycle and embrace forgiveness.

I forgave anyone that had hurt me in anyway or form.

And most importtly, I forgave myself. I had carried guilt and self-blame for far too long. I realized that I was only human, prone to mistakes and imperfections. By forgiving myself, I set myself free from the chains of self-doubt and self-punishment.

I realized that holding onto resentment would only keep me trapped in the past. So, with a brave and open heart, I chose forgiveness.

My life suddenly started to make sense again. The pieces of the puzzle fit together, and I realized that every experience, every challenge had led me to this moment of clarity.

I finished my school year at "Colegio Bíblico Cristiano" and found myself surrounded by remarkable Christian friends, I became best friends with Claudia and Marielvis.

Through their unwavering faith, they taught me the true essence of love, kindness, and compassion. Their support and genuine friendship made me realize that I was never alone in my journey.

The journey of faith is not without its obstacles, but I learned to overcome them with grace and resilience. We faced trials and tribulations, yet we stood firm in our belief that our purpose was greater than any adversity we encountered.

I understood as a new believer was that everyone has their own unique purpose in life. Just as each snowflake is distinct, so too are our individual callings and contributions to the world. It is crucial to remember that God has created each of us with specific talents, gifts, and passions, and He desires for us to use them to serve Him and others.

Discovering your purpose in serving God may take time and patience. It is a journey of self-discovery, seeking God's guidance, and growing in faith. Your purpose may be to serve through acts of kindness, evangelism, teaching, music, or countless other ways. Embrace your uniqueness and trust that God will guide you to the path He has prepared for you.

One day, as I returned home from school, a sense of anticipation filled my heart. Little did I know that this day would mark a turning point in my life, a moment that would set me on a path towards my dreams.

Remember the preacher that prophesied over my life that I was returning to the United states?

I received the news that my visa was ready. My heart leaped with joy, for I knew that this was the fulfillment of the preacher's prophecy. It was as if the universe had conspired to align all the pieces of my life, paving the way for this incredible opportunity.

In that moment, I realized that this was not just a mere coincidence; it was a divine intervention, a manifestation of my unwavering belief and the power of God.

I believed that God had a purpose for every single experience I have encountered along my journey. As I reflect upon the trials and triumphs that have shaped me into the person I am today, I am filled with a deep sense of gratitude and awe for the divine wisdom that guided me through it all.

In the moments of darkness and despair, when life seemed unbearable, it was God's purpose that provided me with the strength to persevere. Each obstacle I faced was a stepping stone towards a greater purpose, teaching me valuable lessons and molding my character.

God's purpose was not to shield me from pain or hardship, but rather to refine my spirit and empower me to become the best version of myself. Each tear shed, each moment of doubt, was a necessary step towards my growth and transformation. The challenges I faced were not meant to break me, but to mold me into a vessel of love, compassion, and strength, Returning back to the Dominican Republic was like a pilgrimage for me. It was more than just a visit to my motherland; it was a spiritual awakening, a divine rendezvous with the Almighty.

Today, I express my deep gratitude for the transformative experience I had in the Dominican Republic. It was a journey that not only brought me face-to-face with myself, but also allowed me to encounter God in a profound and life-changing way, to have witnessed the beauty and brokenness, and to have met God in the midst of it all.

I am so grateful for the lessons learned, the perspectives gained, and the faith that has been strengthened.

The Dominican Republic became a classroom for me, teaching me invaluable lessons about gratitude, compassion, and the true meaning of faith.

I realized that my own struggles and worries paled in comparison to those faced by others, and it was through this realization that I truly surrendered myself to God.

After four years in the Dominican Republic, I finally returned to the United States, I can't even begin to express how grateful I fel

The United States holds a special place in my heart, and I was beyond excited to be reunited with my loved ones and to embar on a new chapter in my life.

I couldn't contain my excitement as I boarded the plane back to the United States. The anticipation of returning to my home country filled me with an overwhelming sense of joy and happiness. As the plane touched down on familiar soil, I couldn' help but feel a rush of emotions coursing through me.

Stepping off the plane, I took a deep breath, inhaling the familia scent of my homeland. It felt like a warm embrace, welcoming m back with open arms. The sights and sounds of the bustling airport filled me with a sense of belonging, as if I had finally con back to where I truly belonged.

Driving through the streets, I couldn't help but appreciate the little things that I had missed. The convenience of everything, th efficiency, and the ease of communication were all things I had taken for granted before. Now, they felt like luxuries I could full appreciate.

Reconnecting with my loved ones was a truly heartwarming experience. The hugs, laughter, and shared stories made me fee like I had never been away. The bond we had built over the yea remained unbreakable, and being back with them brought a sen of completeness to my life.

But one of the biggest adjustments I had to make was going to high school. After spending several years in a different country, it felt strange to be surrounded by a new group of classmates and teachers. However, I quickly settled in and found my place in the school community. In Abraham Lincoln High School , the teachers were supportive and helped me navigate through the challenges of transitioning back into the American education system.

High school was a whirlwind of new experiences and opportunities. I joined clubs, I saw some of my old friends from elementary school, and made some incredible friends along the way, my best friend was Navi she became like my sister. We barely talk, but she will always have a special place in my heart.

But it was an interesting transition, especially during my high school years. It was like stepping into a whole new world a world filled with parties, social events, and a vibrant teenage culture that I hadn't fully experienced before. I was suddenly exposed to a fast-paced environment where socializing and going out seemed to be the norm. It felt like everyone was constantly planning parties, get-togethers, and other events. Initially, I was taken aback by the intensity and frequency of these social activities. However, as time went on, I found myself embracing this new aspect of American high school culture. I started attending parties and getting involved in the social scene. I also started dating.

My first boyfriend was Kenny which I deeply fell in love with in High School, but he was not a good influence.
I learned that the hard way.

Years later while working as a cleaner at a gym called La Fitness, I met my first husband and my life changed in the most beautiful way. My husband and I were lucky to live a wonderful life together with ups and downs. He had a fantastic job that not only met our needs but also allowed us to enjoy many of life's pleasures. He was not only a provider, but also my biggest supporter and believer in my abilities. His unwavering trust in me gave me the confidence to make a significant change in my career. I had felt dissatisfied with my job as a cleaner and without direction. However, with his encouragement and motivation, I took a leap of faith and started working as a bank teller and since then I have worked in banks. Our journey together also led us to the happy moment when we welcomed our son, Liam, into the world, who is the light of our lives.

But unfortunately he was deported to Mexico.

When he was suddenly deported, I felt like he had lost a part of myself. But in the midst of the tears and pain, I found a strength within me that I never knew existed. I realized that wallowing in self-pity would get me nowhere. He had to make a decision. Whether to let this situation consume me or to get over it. And so, I made a conscious decision to become stronger than ever. Through this challenging time, I discovered my own resilience and inner strength. I realized that I could overcome any obstacle that came my way.

Since my husband had his parents and had a house and I decided to take my son to Mexico to live with his father while I adjusted to this situation.

When my son and I first arrived in Mexico, it was a completely new world for us. Liam, being the resilient and adaptable kid that he is, quickly made friends and began to immerse himself in Mexican culture.

Living in Mexico gave Liam a unique opportunity to learn a new language and grow with love. He eagerly accepted the challenge and soon learned to speak Spanish fluently. It was incredible to witness his growth and see him communicate effortlessly. He often returned home excitedly sharing stories about his adventures, new friends, and the fascinating Mexican traditions he had come to love. As a mother and from all the experiences I went through, it was both touching and bittersweet to see Liam blossom in Mexico. I didn't want him to go through the difficulties and challenges that I faced while he was growing up. I wanted him to have a different, perhaps easier, path in life. But it has been heartwarming to witness the immense love and support he has received from his father's family. Since we arrived, they welcomed him with open arms, treating him with a lot of love. They became his support system, his cheerleaders, and his biggest fans. They made him feel like he belonged and was special. Watching him bond with his grandparents, aunts, uncles and cousins, even his neighbors, has been a truly beautiful experience.

They have showered him with love, care and guidance and also shared his traditions, stories and values with him, enriching his cultural identity in ways he could never have imagined. They have become an integral part of his life, transforming him into the incredible person he is today and I couldn't be more grateful.

After my husband's deportation and the difficult decision to take my son Liam to Mexico, I knew our journey was far from over. Determined to give us a better future, I returned to the United States with a heart full of hope and the determination to make a positive change. At the same time, when I returned, I faced numerous challenges that seemed insurmountable. However, I refused to let these obstacles define me or stop me. I knew I had to take control of my life and create a better path for Liam and me. I started working not just one, but two jobs. I was working my dream job day shift at the Credit Union and night shift as a Customer Service Specialist, working tirelessly pushing myself to the limit to ensure we could meet our basic needs and alleviate the debt we owed. It was not easy. The days were long and the nights even longer, but I never lost sight of my ultimate goal: to provide a stable and safe home for my son. Through hard work, perseverance and unwavering determination, I managed to pay off all the debt that was weighing us down. It was a long and arduous journey, but every sacrifice was worth it for the opportunity to create a better future for Liam and me. I laughed today, but I remember growing up, I faced a number of challenges that made me feel like no one believed in me, not even my own family. It was discouraging to constantly hear my aunts (not all of them) whisper about me, doubt my potential, and say that I would never amount to anything or that "I wasn't going to be nothing" that's how ugly they expressed themselves about me. I always remember that day when I found them talking bad about me and it just makes me laugh. Here I am today, standing tall and proud, all thanks to the glory of God.

On that magical day of May 25, 2018, I achieved a milestone I had only previously dreamed of. I bought my own house. The feeling of accomplishment and pride that came over me was indescribable. It was a symbol of all the hard work, resilience and sacrifices he had made.

In that moment, I realized that no challenge is too great when you have the strength to persevere. The road to success is not always smooth, but it is in those moments of adversity that we discover our true strength and resilience. I am living proof that with determination and unwavering faith, we can overcome any obstacle and achieve our dreams.

Today, as I sit in the comfort of my own home writing this book, I am reminded of the journey that brought us here. am grateful for the lessons learned, the strength gained, and the unwavering belief in myself that carried us through the toughest of times.

To all those facing challenges, I implore you to never lose hope. Believe in God and in yourself, work hard, and never give up. Your dreams are within reach, even if they seem distant at the moment. Remember, every setback is an opportunity for a comeback.

Life may throw unexpected curveballs our way, but it is our response to these challenges that defines us. Embrace the journey, for it is through the struggles that we find our true potential. Be resilient, be courageous, and always keep moving forward, knowing that you have the power to create a better future for yourself and your loved ones.

Believe in the power of your dreams, and never forget that you are capable of achieving greatness. Your story is still being written, and the best chapters are yet to come, but you have to let God write your story.

In life there's also, unexpected turns and challenges can often lead us down paths we never imagined.

One such journey began when Liam's dad and I sadly decided to part ways, leading me to bring my son back from Mexico. While the circumstances may have changed, our bond as a family remains unbreakable.

It is essential to remember that love knows no boundaries. Although our family dynamic has shifted, the love that flows between Liam, his dad, and myself is unwavering. We have chosen to rise above our differences and focus on what truly matters – the happiness and well-being of our remarkable son.

Throughout this journey, I have discovered that family extends far beyond blood relations. Liam's extended family has embraced me with open arms, and his sisters have become a source of joy and support in our lives. Their presence has been nothing short of a blessing, reminding me that love and acceptance can be found in the most unexpected places.

Life has taught me that family is not defined by marital status or geographical location. It is defined by the love, care, and support we extend to one another.

In the midst of this challenging chapter, I once again learned the power of forgiveness and the importance of cherishing every moment.

Life is too short to hold onto resentment or dwell on what could have been. Instead, I choose to focus on the incredible journey that lies ahead for Liam, his dad, and myself.

Instead I am filled with gratitude for the lessons learned and the love that continues to bind us together.

When I reflect on my decision to get married at 19, I am filled with gratitude for the courage I had at that time. It takes a certain level of maturity and fearlessness to make such a commitment at a young age. I am thankful for the love and support I received from my partner during that period of my life. Those years taught me so much about communication, compromise, and the true meaning of partnership.

Becoming a parent at a young age was an unexpected blessing. While it certainly presented its own set of challenges, I am grateful for the lessons it taught me about responsibility, selflessness, and unconditional love. The joy and fulfillment I experienced as a parent are beyond words. It allowed me to grow in ways I never thought possible and gave my life a purpose that I cherish.

Although my marriage ultimately ended in divorce, I still feel a sense of gratitude for that experience as well. It was a painful and difficult process, but it taught me the importance of self-reflection, personal growth, and the ability to let go when necessary. Divorce, as heartbreaking as it can be, opened doors to new possibilities and allowed me to prioritize my own happiness and well-being.

After my divorce, I embarked on a journey to find love once again. It hasn't been an easy road, but I have had the opportunity to date and meet some incredible individuals along the way. Out of all the people I have encountered, there are two individuals who have left a lasting impression on my heart, the Italian man who I felt in love with, and Kevin, whose untimely passed away in a car accident shattered my world.

Ever since I was a little girl, I always dreamed of dating an Italian. There was something about their culture, charm, and passion that captivated me from a young age. The Italian guy taught me the importance of embracing love with all its complexities and reminded me of the power of vulnerability. I just felt right with him in every way. However, life has a way of throwing unexpected curveballs. Tragedy struck when I met Kevin, we were building a beautiful connection, but fate had different plans, and Kevin's life was cut short in a tragic car accident. Losing him was a devastating blow, leaving me with a void that seemed impossible to fill.

The saddest part was that I was with him that night and even went to the hospital hoping he would be ok. The news of Kevin's passing shook me to my core. Days turned into weeks, and weeks into months, but the pain remained, a constant reminder of the void left by his absence. In the midst of my own grief, I was blindsided by the unexpected backlash from Kevin's family. They began to harbor suspicions that I had somehow contributed to his untimely death, but I did not have anything to do with what happened to him that night. I forgive them and may He Rest In Peace.

Now, as I look ahead, I hold onto hope that love will find its way back into my life. I've always had this heartfelt prayer, a plea to God to let me experience true love before I leave this world.

"

Months later life took an unexpected turn. I also found myself involved in a car accident, facing the very real possibility of losing my own life.

In the aftermath of the accident, I felt a mix of gratitude, fear, and disbelief. Gratitude because I was still alive, breathing and able to see another day and most importantly see my son. I couldn't help but count my blessings and feel an immense sense of appreciation for the second chance I had been given.

I also cannot express enough how grateful I am to the person who found me in the car accident. They truly saved my life. I cannot imagine what would have happened if they had not come to my rescue. Their quick thinking and selflessness are something I will never forget.

Through the darkness of that accident, I discovered the true value of life. Every breath, every heartbeat, and every moment became precious beyond measure. I realized that life is a gift, a fleeting opportunity that should never be taken for granted. I began to cherish each day, no longer willing to waste a single second on negativity or trivial matters. My faith once again became my guiding light. I found solace in knowing that there is a higher power, a force that watches over us and provides strength when we need it most. I turned to my faith as a source of comfort, finding peace in the midst of chaos. It taught me to trust in the journey, even when it seems uncertain, and to have faith in the power of resilience. But above all, it was my family that truly anchored me during this challenging time. My cousin Andia, My good friend Mike, and my Aunt became my pillars of support, offering unwavering love and encouragement.

As I reflect, I see that sometimes we forget to appreciate the incredible gift that life truly is. We get so caught up in our own worries, stresses, and desires that we fail to recognize the beauty and abundance that surrounds us. It's easy to take things for granted. Our health, our loved ones, our opportunities, and lose sight of just how fortunate we are to be here. If I would have lost my life in that car accident I would have never seen my son again.

But we often find ourselves chasing after the next big thing, believing that true happiness lies in achieving our goals or acquiring material possessions. We become consumed by a constant need for more – more money, more success, more recognition. We believe that once we attain these things, we will finally be content. But the truth is, life is not about accumulating things or reaching certain milestones; it's about cherishing every moment and being grateful for what we already have.

Gratitude is a powerful force that can transform our perspective and bring immense joy into our lives. When we practice gratitude, we shift our focus from what is lacking to what is present. We begin to notice the little things – a warm smile, a beautiful sunset, a good cup of coffee – and realize that these simple pleasures make life truly worth living.

Being grateful doesn't mean that we ignore our problems or pretend that everything is perfect. It simply means that we choose to appreciate the good, even amidst the challenges. It means acknowledging that life is a precious gift, filled with both ups and downs, and finding the silver lining in every situation.

So, as you navigate the ups and downs of your own journey, remember the value of life. Embrace each day with gratitude, hold tightly to your faith, and cherish the love and support of our family. Life is a beautiful journey filled with ups and downs, twists and turns, and unexpected detours. It can sometimes feel overwhelming, especially when faced with challenges and uncertainties. But in these moments, it's essential to hold on to faith and trust in something greater than ourselves.

Trust in God's Plan. Remember that you are not alone in this journey. There is a divine plan at work, and everything happens for a reason. Even when things seem tough, have faith that God has a purpose for your life. Trust that He will guide you through the ups and downs and lead you to where you need to be.

Life is full of uncertainties, and it's natural to feel anxious or overwhelmed by them. However, instead of resisting the unknown, embrace it with faith. Have confidence that God is in control, and He will provide you with the strength and wisdom to navigate through the challenges that come your way.

Remember, faith is not about having all the answers or avoiding challenges. It's about believing in something greater than yourself and trusting in God's plan for your life. Embrace the journey, knowing that your faith will carry you through the ups and downs.

Have faith, and trust in the beautiful path that lies ahead.

Part Three

Blooming With Love and Grace

Today as a Banking Specialist and Author

My 9 year old son and I

When I first started working as a Banking Specialist

My first Banking Job as a Teller

Chapter 9

Stepping into Radiance

I have discovered a radiant light that shines brighter than ever. It is within this new radiance that I have embraced the beauty of living a new me. With every step I take, I am filled with an unwavering sense of inspiration and determination, propelling me toward a life of infinite possibilities. Leaving everything that happened to me in the past has been one of the most empowering decisions I have ever made. It's amazing how a simple change of perspective can completely transform your life and free you from the chains of the past. Letting go of burdens, regrets, and painful memories has allowed me to embrace the present moment and create a better future for myself. Gone are the days of doubts and limiting beliefs. I have shed the layers of negativity that once weighed me down and, in their place, have cultivated a garden of self-love and self-acceptance. Every morning when the sun rises, I am reminded that I too have the power to overcome any challenge that comes my way.

Living a new self means embracing authenticity with open arms. I have learned to celebrate my uniqueness and accept my flaws, because they are what make me wonderfully human.
no longer seek validation from others, because I have realized that the only validation I need is God's and my own.

I am enough, just as I am.

I have cultivated a deep connection with my passions and dreams. I have unearthed hidden talents and pursued interests that set my soul on fire. With each pursuit, my spirit soars, and I am reminded of the boundless potential that lies within me. I am no longer confined by societal expectations. Instead, I am guided by my own intuition and inner wisdom. Living a new me also means cherishing the relationships that uplift and support me. I have surrounded myself with kindred souls who inspire me to be the best version of myself. Together, we create a tapestry of love, encouragement, and growth. We lift each other up, celebrating victories and providing solace in times of struggle.

There comes a time when we must summon the courage to leave the past behind and embrace the radiant future that awaits us. It is in this moment of transformation that we find the true essence of our being, and discover the limitless potential that resides within us.

Leaving the past behind is not always an easy task. It requires us to let go of the comfortable familiarity that we have grown accustomed to and venture into the unknown. But it is in this unknown territory that the magic happens – where growth, liberation, and self-discovery flourish.

When we release the shackles of the past, we liberate ourselves from the burdens that have held us back. We shed the weight of regrets, disappointments, and missed opportunities, and make room for the brilliance of the present moment. It is in this newfound freedom that we can truly step into our radiance.

As we embark on this journey of leaving the past behind, it is important to remember that we are not defined by our past experiences. We are not limited by our failures or defined by our mistakes. Instead, we are shaped by the lessons we have learned and the strength we have gained along the way.

Each step we take towards leaving the past behind brings us closer to our authentic selves. It allows us to embrace our true passions, dreams, and aspirations. It enables us to rewrite our story and create a future that is filled with love, joy, and fulfillment.

In this process, it is crucial to surround ourselves with positivity and inspiration. We must seek out mentors, guides, and companions who uplift and support us on our journey. Their encouragement and wisdom will provide us with the strength and motivation we need to push forward, even when faced with challenges.

Leaving the past behind is not a one-time event, but rather a continuous practice. It requires us to constantly reassess our beliefs, behaviors, and patterns, and make choices that align with our highest self. It is through this ongoing commitment to growth that we will continue to radiate our true essence to the world.

Remember that the power to create a radiant future lies within you. Embrace the unknown, let go of what no longer serves you, and step into the brilliance of your authentic self.

Chapter 10

Cultivating Gratitude and finding Joy

In the beautiful journey of life, there are moments that leave us breathless, moments that fill our hearts with a sense of wonder and gratitude. These moments, though seemingly fleeting, hold the power to transform our entire perspective and bring us closer to true happiness. It is within these moments that we realize the importance of cultivating gratitude and finding joy, for they are the keys to unlocking a life filled with abundance and contentment.

As I said before gratitude is a powerful tool that allows us to recognize and appreciate the blessings that surround us each and every day. It is a mindset that shifts our focus from what we lack to what we have, from what went wrong to what went right. When we cultivate gratitude, we open ourselves up to a world of possibilities and become more aware of the beauty that exists within the smallest details of our lives.

Finding joy is an art that requires us to look beyond the surface, to dig deep within ourselves and embrace the present moment. It is a choice to see the silver linings in every situation, no matter how challenging it may be. Joy is not a destination, but a state of being that can be found in the simplest of pleasures – a warm hug, a heartfelt laugh, a quiet moment of reflection.

But how do we cultivate gratitude and find joy amidst the chaos and uncertainty of life?

t begins by practicing mindfulness, being fully present and aware of our thoughts, emotions, and surroundings. When we are mindful, we can better appreciate the beauty of the present moment and let go of worries about the future or regrets from the past.

Another way to cultivate gratitude is by keeping a gratitude journal. Each day, take a moment to reflect on three things you are grateful for. It could be as simple as the sun shining through your window, the sound of birds chirping, or the warm cup of coffee in your hands. By consciously acknowledging these blessings, we train our minds to focus on the positive aspects of our lives.

By the way, this is how I started writing, as I immersed myself in the art of journaling, something magical started to happen. Words that were once scattered fragments began to take shape, forming sentences that resonated with meaning. Ideas blossomed, intertwining with heartfelt experiences and transforming into narratives waiting to be shared. It was as if my journal became a breeding ground for creativity, a fertile ground where stories were born.

With every entry, I discovered the power of my voice and the strength of my words. I realized that my thoughts had value, and they deserved to be heard. Journaling became a catalyst for self-discovery, enabling me to explore the depths of my imagination and uncover hidden treasures within my own mind.

Through the act of recording my daily life, I unearthed a multitude of storylines that begged to be expanded upon. My journal became a roadmap, guiding me on the path towards writing books. It taught me discipline, as I committed to writing every day, honing my skills and refining my craft. It served as a reminder that writing is not just a hobby but a lifelong commitment, a way of life.

Journaling allowed me to navigate the peaks and valleys of my creative journey. It became my refuge during moments of self-doubt and my confidant when inspiration seemed to wane. It provided solace in times of uncertainty, reminding me that even the smallest of ideas can spark a flame of creativity.

Today, as I hold my published books in my hands, I am reminded of the humble beginnings that led me here. I am grateful for the journaling practice that shaped me as a writer, for it was through the pages of my journal that I discovered my voice, my purpose, and my passion. Finding joy, on the other hand, requires us to engage in activities that bring us genuine happiness. It could be pursuing a hobby, spending time with loved ones, or simply takin a walk in nature. When we make time for things that truly light u up, we invite joy into our lives and create a ripple effect that spreads positivity to those around us.

Remember, cultivating gratitude and finding joy is a lifelong journey, one that requires patience, perseverance, and a willingnes to embrace the ups and downs of life. It is not about denying the challenges that come our way, but rather about choosing to find the silver linings and focusing on the things that bring us happiness.

Chapter 11

Living a purposeful life

My life has a purpose, a purpose that drives me to get up every morning with determination and passion. No matter how difficult the road is, I know that I am here for a reason, and that reason is to leave a positive mark on this world. I am a testimony to the incredible power of God's grace and guidance in my life. I am a Mother, a Banking Specialist and an Author, all for the glory of God.

As a Mother, I have been blessed with the privilege of witnessing the miracle of life unfold before my eyes and fill my heart with an overwhelming sense of joy and responsibility. Through the sleepless nights, the tender moments, and the daily sacrifices, I am reminded of God's unconditional love and the immense strength he has given me.

In my role as a Banking Specialist, I have been given the opportunity to positively impact the financial well-being of others. I strive to provide guidance, support and sound advice to those seeking to manage their resources wisely. With every transaction, I am reminded of the abundance God has blessed us with and the responsibility to steward it well. It is through my work that I am able to demonstrate integrity, honesty and compassion, reflecting the character of God in every interaction.

As an Author, I have been given a platform to share my thoughts, experiences, and insights with the world. Through the written word, I seek to inspire, uplift, and encourage others on their journey of faith. Whether it be through a devotional, a blog post, or a heartfelt post on my Instagram. I aim to shine a light on the beauty and goodness that surrounds us, reminding others of God's presence in every aspect of our lives.

Today, I am humbled and grateful for the multifaceted roles I have been blessed to fulfill. I recognize that it is not by my own strength or abilities that I am able to succeed, but through the grace and favor of God. I am reminded that in all that I do, whether it be Motherhood, Banking, or Writing, it is ultimately for His glory. I strive to honor Him through my actions, seeking His guidance and wisdom to navigate each step of my journey.

In the midst of life's darkest moments, when despair seems to overshadow any glimmer of light, remember that there is always hope. Even when everything around us seems to crumble, there is a powerful force that can lift us up and guide us towards a brighter tomorrow. That force is none other than God.

God, the source of all love and compassion, is always there for us, ready to embrace us in our times of struggle. He understands our pain, our fears, and our doubts, and He offers us solace and strength. When we feel lost, He is the steady hand that guides us back on the right path. When we feel broken, He is the gentle touch that heals our wounds and restores our spirits.

It is in the moments of darkness that our faith is truly tested, but it is also in these moments that we can witness the power of God's love and grace. His light shines brightest in the darkest of times, illuminating our paths and leading us towards a future filled with hope and renewal.

Let us remember that He is our refuge and our strength, an ever-present help in times of trouble. Let us trust in His divine plan, knowing that He works all things for our good. Let us have faith that, just as the night gives way to the dawn, our current struggles will give way to a brighter tomorrow.

And when hope seems elusive, let us seek solace in prayer. Pour out your heart to God, for He is a loving listener who longs to ease your burdens. He is always with you, ready to offer comfort and guidance, even in the darkest of moments. Trust that His love is greater than any obstacle you may face, and that through Him, all things are possible.

Even as I reflect upon my own life journey, I am reminded of the incredible moments that have shaped me and guided me towards the person I am destined to become.

From when I discovered that the woman I had affectionately called "Mama Luisa" was not my biological mother. This revelation shook the very foundation of my identity, leaving me with questions and uncertainties.

The day I met my mom for the first time will forever be etched in my memory. It was a moment of connection and understanding, all the missing puzzle pieces of my life.

The next chapter of my journey took me to the United States, a land of opportunity and endless possibilities where I was adopted

The bittersweer moment of when I returned to the Dominican Republic, was depressed, but I found God's solace, guidance, and a profound sense of purpose. I discovered that I was never alone, that even in the darkest of moments, there was a guiding light that illuminated the path ahead. In those difficult times, I also recognize the strength within me that allowed me to persevere.

While the pain of my past still lingers, I have learned to accept it as a part of my journey. It has shaped me into the person I am today, and I am determined to use my experiences to help others who may be going through similar struggles. Through sharing my story, I hope to inspire others to seek help, to reach out, and to never lose hope.

Life is a series of ups and downs, and it is in our darkest moments that we often discover our true strength. I am no longer defined by the sadness I once felt, but by the resilience and courage I have found within.

Looking back on my life journey, again I am just filled with gratitude for every twist and turn that has brought me to where I am today. It is through the challenges and hardships that I have grown, learned, and discovered my true strength. Each experience, whether joyous or painful, has shaped me into the resilient and compassionate individual I am proud to be.

In the grand tapestry of existence, we are all woven together with a unique purpose. Each one of us holds within us the power to make a difference, to create ripples that reverberate far beyond our own lives. It is through living a purposeful life that we truly shine and radiate our inner essence.

Living with purpose is about aligning our actions with our values, dreams, and passions. It is about embracing our authenticity and using our unique gifts and talents to contribute to the world around us. When we live with purpose, life becomes a canvas on which we paint strokes of love, kindness, and inspiration.

Often, the path to living a purposeful life begins with self-reflection. Taking the time to delve deep into our hearts and minds, we can uncover our true passions and desires. What ignites a fire within us? What brings us joy and fulfillment? These questions guide us towards our purpose, our North Star that leads us forward.

Living a purposeful life means stepping out of our comfort zones, for it is in the realm of the unknown that we discover our true potential. It requires us to embrace challenges and face our fears head-on. It is in these moments of growth that we truly bloom, transforming ourselves into the best versions of who we can be.

Living with purpose also means cultivating a mindset of gratitude. Gratitude opens our hearts and minds to the abundance that surrounds us. It allows us to appreciate the beauty in the simplest of things and to recognize the interconnectedness of all beings. With gratitude as our compass, we navigate through life with a sense of wonder and awe. Moreover, living a purposeful life is not just about personal fulfillment, but also about making a positive impact on others. It is about reaching out a helping hand to those in need, spreading love and compassion wherever we go. By uplifting others, we become a beacon of light, illuminating the path for those who may have lost their way.

It is not easy. There will be moments of doubt and uncertainty, moments when we stumble and fall. But it is in these moments that we must remind ourselves of our purpose, our reason for being. We must summon the strength within us to rise again, to persevere, and to continue moving forward.

Chapter 12

Embracing the unknown and trusting God

In life, we often find ourselves embracing the unknown. It's like walking on a path without seeing what lies ahead. It can be scary, but also exciting. However, despite the uncertainties, we can always trust in God. He gives us the strength to face the unknown with courage and determination.
Throughout my life, there is no doubt that life was testing my strength and endurance. However, I now realize that each and every one of these experiences was a valuable lesson in disguise.

Life has a way of teaching us the lessons we need to learn, even if they come in the form of difficulties. It is through these tests that we discover our true strength and potential. Every struggle serves as an opportunity for growth and personal improvement. In the face of adversity, I have learned the importance of perseverance. I have discovered the power of resilience, of moving forward even when the road seems insurmountable. It is during these difficult times that our true character and determination shine.

Every setback has taught me the value of patience. I have learned that success does not come overnight, but through constant effort and unwavering dedication. The journey may be long and arduous, but with patience we will eventually reach the desired destination.

Moreover, every disappointment has taught me the significance of gratitude. It is easy to take things for granted when everything is going smoothly, but when faced with disappointment, we realize the true value of what we have. Gratitude allows us to appreciate the present moment and find joy in even the smallest victories.

Above all, these lessons have taught me the importance of self-belief. In times of doubt and uncertainty, it is crucial to trust in oneself and have faith in our abilities. We possess an inner strength that can carry us through any storm, as long as we believe in ourselves and our potential.

In the quiet moments of self-reflection, I can't help but feel like I'm not quite where I'm supposed to be. It's not a feeling of discontent or despair, but rather a deep-rooted sense of ambition and a longing to achieve all the dreams that dance within my heart.

I have so many aspirations, so many goals that I yearn to accomplish. They sparkle in my mind like distant stars, waiting to be grasped and brought into my reality. And I firmly believe that with the help of God, I will manifest these dreams and turn them into tangible achievements.

Each day, I wake up with a renewed determination to make progress towards these goals. I remind myself that life is a journey, and that every step I take, no matter how small, brings me closer to my destination. Sometimes, it's easy to lose sight of this truth and become overwhelmed by the enormity of my dreams. But I'm learning to trust the process and have faith in my abilities.

I've come to realize that life is not about reaching a specific destination, but rather about the journey itself. It's about the lessons learned along the way, the growth experienced, and the person I become in the pursuit of my dreams. It's about embracing each challenge as an opportunity for growth and using setbacks as stepping stones towards success.

I know that the road ahead may be filled with obstacles and uncertainties, but I choose to face them head-on. I understand that success is not guaranteed, but I am determined to give my all and never give up. I believe that every dream I have is within my reach, and I am willing to work tirelessly to make them a reality.

So, I may not be where I'm supposed to be just yet, but I am on my way. With God by my side, I have the strength and guidance to overcome any obstacle that stands in my path. I am confident that as long as I continue to dream, set goals, and take action, I will reach heights that I never thought possible.

In the end, it's not about the destination, but the journey. And I am grateful for every step I take towards my dreams, for it is through this journey that I am becoming the person I was always meant to be.

There are countless moments when we find ourselves standing at the crossroads of uncertainty. The path ahead seems hazy, and we are left grappling with the unknown. It is during these moments that we must learn to embrace the unknow and trust in God's divine plan.

Embracing the unknown may seem daunting at first, but it is in these uncharted territories that we find growth, strength, and incredible opportunities. It is where we discover our hidden potential and realize that our capacity to overcome challenges knows no bounds. Instead of fearing the unknown, let us welcome it with open arms, for it is in the midst of uncertainty that we truly learn to live.

In our journey of embracing the unknown, it is essential to trust in God's guidance and wisdom. He is the compass that points us in the right direction, and the pillar of strength that supports us through every twist and turn. When we trust in God, we relinquish our worries and anxieties, knowing that He holds the blueprint of our lives.

Trusting God does not mean that everything will unfold exactly as we envision. It means having faith that even in the face of adversity, God has a purpose for us. It means surrendering our desires and aligning ourselves with His divine will. For it is when we let go and trust in His plan that we find peace, contentment, and a renewed sense of purpose.

So, let us embrace the unknown and trust in God's unwavering love and guidance. Let us release our fears and doubts, and instead, cultivate a spirit of courage and resilience. For in doing so, we open ourselves up to a world of endless possibilities and embark on a journey of growth and self-discovery.

Remember, when we embrace the unknown and trust in God, we tap into a wellspring of strength that resides within us. We become the heroes of our own stories, facing each new chapter with a spirit of anticipation and unwavering faith. So, let us step forward with confidence, knowing that we are never alone, for God is walking beside us every step of the way.

Embrace the unknown, and trust in God's divine plan.

We were not just made to live and die; we were made for a purpose. Each and every one of us has a unique role to fulfill in this world. We have talents, passions, and dreams that are waiting to be discovered and pursued. But finding our purpose can sometimes feel like an uphill battle, especially when we face obstacles and uncertainties along the way.

When we ask God to guide us, we are acknowledging that we need divine wisdom and guidance to fulfill our purpose. It's a humble recognition that we cannot do it all on our own, and that we need the help of a higher power to lead us towards our true calling.

But how do we open the door to fulfillment and leave a lasting impact on the world around us?

The first step is to listen to the whispers of our hearts. Deep within each of us lies a unique calling, a true north that guides us toward our purpose. It can be a passion, a talent or a desire to make a difference. Take a moment to silence the noise of the world and truly listen to what your heart is telling you. It may be a faint murmur at first, but with patience and perseverance it will become louder and clearer.

Once you've discovered your purpose, embrace it with unwavering determination. Let it light a fire within you, propelling you forward even in the face of adversity. Remember, a purposeful life is not without challenges, but rather is a testament to our resilience and strength. Embrace the lessons that come with each obstacle, knowing that they are mere stepping stones on the path to greatness.

Never underestimate the power of connection and community. Surround yourself with like-minded people who share your vision and values. Together, you can uplift, inspire, and create ripple effect that goes far beyond your own journey. Collaborate, support and celebrate each other's victories, because a purposeful life is not a solitary endeavor but a collective celebration of the human spirit.

In the pursuit of a purposeful life, it is crucial to cultivate a mindset of gratitude and abundance. Count your blessings, no matter how small, and let gratitude be the fuel that propels you forward. Cherish the present moment and find joy in the simple pleasures that life offers.

never forget about God, and that a purposeful life is not solely about personal fulfillment but also about serving others. Find ways to contribute to the well-being of those around you, whether through acts of kindness, volunteering, or dedicating your talents to a greater cause. By giving back, you not only enrich the lives of others but also create a sense of purpose that transcends your own existence.

And never forget the power of praying. That simple prayer in the Dominican Republic saved my life.

I was once lost in the vast abyss of depression, a prisoner of my own thoughts and emotions. The weight of the world seemed to crush my spirit, leaving me feeling empty, broken, and devoid of any sense of identity. It was as if I had lost myself along the way, and I had no idea how to find my way back.

But in my darkest hour, when I had no strength left to fight, I turned to prayers. I poured out my heart, my fears, and my pain to a higher power, surrendering myself completely to the divine presence that I believed could heal me. And in that moment, something miraculous happened.

A prayer saved my life. She taught me that even in the midst of despair, there is always a glimmer of hope. She showed me that no matter how broken I felt, I was never truly alone.

Never underestimate the power of a sincere prayer.

In life, there are times when we find ourselves on the brink of despair, when everything seems to fall apart around us and hope becomes nothing more than a distant memory. It is in these moments of pure desperation that a prayer can be our saving grace, our guiding light in the darkest of times.

Just as a prayer saved me from depression, illness, a car accident, and many other challenges, a prayer can save you too. Embrace the power of prayer and let it weave its magic into your life.

If you find yourself lost in the depths of despair, I urge you to turn to prayer. Allow yourself to be vulnerable, open your heart and pour out your deepest desires. Trust that there is a power beyond your understanding that hears you, loves you, and is ready to lift you up.

I want to take a moment and say a prayer for you.

Prayer

Heavenly Father ,

We come before you today, humbly seeking your forgiveness for any mistakes or wrongdoings we may have committed. We acknowledge that we are imperfect beings, prone to making errors in judgment and action. Please forgive us for any hurt we may have caused others, knowingly or unknowingly. Grant us the strength to learn from our mistakes and to strive to be better individuals each day.

We also ask for your guidance in our lives. Life can be full of uncertainties and challenges, and sometimes it's hard to know which path to take. Please illuminate our way, showing us the right choices to make and helping us discern what is truly important. May your wisdom guide our decisions and lead us towards a life of purpose and fulfillment.

Lastly, we ask for your abundant love to surround us. Your love is like no other, unconditional and all-encompassing. Please fill our hearts with your love, allowing it to overflow into our relationships, our actions, and our thoughts. Help us to love others as you love us, with kindness, compassion, and understanding.

May we always seek forgiveness, guidance, and love from you, dear God.

Amen.

If we only knew that God's love is unconditional and knows no boundaries. It surpasses any human understanding, for it is a divine love that can heal our deepest wounds and mend broken hearts. When we allow God's love into our lives, we invite a power greater than ourselves to guide us through the darkest of times.

When we take a moment to pause, to breathe, and to invite God's love into our hearts, we realize that we are never alone. God is always with us, ready to uplift us and carry us through life's storms.

In times of despair, it is God's grace that provides us with the strength and courage to persevere. It is through His grace that we find forgiveness, redemption, and the ability to forgive ourselves and others. His grace empowers us to let go of past mistakes and embrace a future filled with hope and second chances.

When we allow God's love and grace into our hearts, we become vessels of His light in a world that often feels consumed by darkness. We can extend that same love and grace to others, offering compassion and understanding in a world that desperately needs it.

Let us not forget that God's love and grace are not reserved for a select few but are available to all who seek it. Regardless of our past, our flaws, or our doubts, God's love is always there, waiting for us to open our hearts and receive it.

Remember, no matter what struggles or challenges we may face, we are not alone. God's love and grace are always there, ready to uplift us, heal us, and guide us. Allow His love to fill your heart, and watch as His grace transforms your life.

So, what life taught me in the last 30 years?

I have learned countless lessons that have shaped me into the person I am today. Through the ups and downs, one important lesson stands out: there is always light at the end of the tunnel. Life has a way of surprising us. Just when we think all is lost, a breakthrough may occur, bringing with it a renewed sense of purpose and joy. It is during these moments that we realize the true power of resilience and the importance of never giving up. From the pain of being abandoned by my mother to the blessings of being raised by my loving grandmother, each experience has shaped me into the person I am today. And amidst the trials of feeling rejected and the rollercoaster of relationships, I have discovered a profound truth that has transformed my existence – the power of forgiveness and the embrace of God. I realized that I had a choice – to let bitterness consume me or to rise above the pain and find strength in my circumstances.

In the arms of my grandmother that I discovered the power of unconditional love, resilience, and the beauty of second chances. She taught me that no matter where we come from or what challenges we face, we have the power within us to create a meaningful and purposeful life.

Relationships, with their joys and sorrows, taught me about vulnerability, trust, and the importance of communication. I learned that true connections are built on a foundation of honesty, respect, and mutual understanding. Through the highs and lows, I came to understand that genuine love requires effort, patience, and the willingness to forgive.

I also learned that sometimes, for our own well-being, it is necessary to say goodbye. That goodbye simply means that we have recognized that our paths have diverged and holding on to something that no longer aligns with our values or goals will only hold us back. It takes courage to free ourselves from what no longer serves us, but doing so opens up opportunities for new, more fulfilling connections to come into our lives.

And when I felt like I had reached my breaking point, I found comfort in the arms of God. It was through this divine connection that I learned the true meaning of grace and the transformative power of faith. With God in my heart, I found the strength to forgive those who had hurt me, and in doing so, I freed myself from the prison of resentment.

Life has a way of teaching us deep truths if we are open to learning. It has taught me that our past does not define us, but rather that it is the decisions we make in the present that shape our future. It has taught me that forgiveness is not a sign of weakness, but rather an act of strength and liberation. It has taught me that no matter how dark the night may seem, there is always a ray of hope waiting to be discovered.

I carry within me the wisdom gained from each experience and am determined to live a life of purpose, love and forgiveness.

So I invite you to also commit to living a life of purpose, love and forgiveness. Don't let anything or anyone stop you on your path to personal fulfillment and happiness.
You deserve the best!

Conclusion

In the final pages of my memoir, I stand in awe of the incredible journey I have been on. It is with a grateful heart that I reflect on how God's love and grace have saved my life.

Throughout these pages, I have shared some of the darkest moments of my existence, the moments when I felt broken and lost. But through it all, God's love shone brightly, guiding me towards a path of healing and redemption.

I have learned that no matter how deep the pit of despair may be, there is always hope. God's love is like a beacon of light, illuminating even the darkest corners of our souls. It is in those moments of surrender that we can experience the true power of His grace.

God's love has taught me the importance of forgiveness, both for others and for myself. It is through forgiveness that we can release the weight of past hurts and find freedom in our hearts. It is through forgiveness that we can truly bloom into the radiant beings we were created to be.

In the midst of my struggles, I have come to understand that God's love is not conditional. It does not require perfection or performance. It is a love that embraces us in our brokenness and whispers words of comfort and healing.

I have witnessed miracles unfold before my very eyes, where God's love has transformed lives and brought about restoration. It is a love that knows no bounds, that reaches into the depths of our souls and breathes life into our weary spirits.

As I conclude this memoir, I urge you, to open your heart to God's love and grace. Allow Him to work in your life, to heal your wounds, and to bring you into a new season of blossoming radiance.

No matter what you may be facing, remember that you are never alone. God's love is always there, waiting to embrace you and guide you towards a life filled with purpose and joy.

May this memoir serve as a testament to the power of God's love and grace. May it inspire you to seek His presence in every moment and to trust in His plan for your life. And may you, too, experience the miraculous transformation that comes from surrendering to His love.

With a heart overflowing with gratitude, I bid you farewell.

May your own journey be filled with the radiance of God's love.

Questions and Answers about Claritza Rausch Peralta

Question: What inspired you to write this memoir?
Answer: I wanted to share my life's journey and the lessons I've learned along the way, in the hope that it may inspire and resonate with others.

Question: What were the major turning points in your life?
Answer: From personal triumphs to unexpected challenges, these moments shaped who I am today.

Question: How did you discover God's love and grace in your life?
Answer: Again throughout my darkest moments, I found solace in prayer and sought guidance from God. His love and grace gradually revealed themselves through small miracles, unexpected support, and the strength to overcome challenges.

Question: How did God's love and grace help you navigate difficult relationships or conflicts?
Answer: God's love and grace taught me the importance of forgiveness and understanding. By extending His love to others, I was able to approach conflicts with a compassionate heart, fostering healing and reconciliation.

Question: Who were the most significant people in your life and how did they shape you?

Answer: My Grandmother " Mama Luisa" was everything to me, she still is. She was my guiding light, my rock, and my confidante. I cherished our moments together, whether it was watching a " Novela" together, walking to church with my "Madrina" Eroina, or making me breakfast and taking me to school "la escuelita"

and Liam my son, being a mother has taught me countless lessons and has truly been a transformative experience. From the moment I held my child in my arms, I realized that parenthood is a journey that is both challenging and rewarding, I love them both so much!

Question: How did your upbringing influence your choices and beliefs?

Answer: Exploring the impact of my family, cultural background, and childhood experiences helped me understand how they shaped my perspective on life.

Question: What are the most memorable experiences in your life and why?

Answer: Growing up with my grandmother was truly one of the most memorable experiences of my life, the encounters I had with God, another unforgettable experience was when I was a little girl, traveling to Puerto Rico with my cousins and praying with them at my "Tia Ana's house, the day I became a parent was undeniably one of the most incredible moments of my life and, finally the day I bought my first house it was a culmination of hard work, determination, and a dream come true, oh I can't forget going out with my best cousins Andia were great times too lol.

Best Memories

Dressing up with my brothers and sister

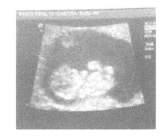

When I found out I was going to be a mother

My adopted dad , son and family celebration christmas

Getting ready to go work at the Bank

Celebrating " Mama Luisa" Birthday

Going out with my favorite cousin

My first time with my biological parents as a family

When I bought my first house

Taking my son to Dominican Republic and show him where I was born

Taking my sister and my biological mother to Philadelphia with our kids

Note to Self

Dear Claritza,

As you celebrate your 30th birthday, I want you to take a moment to reflect on the incredible journey that has brought you here. You have accomplished so much, and I am in awe of the person you have become.

Writing this book was no coincidence; it was a divine plan set in motion by your Heavenly Father. You were chosen to share your story, to inspire others, and to bring light into the lives of those who read your words. Embrace this purpose and know that you are making a difference in the world.

I want you to know just how proud I am of you. Every day, you continue to amaze me with your strength, resilience, and determination. You have faced countless challenges and obstacles, but you have always risen above them. Your ability to overcome adversity is a testament to your character and spirit.

On this special day, I want you to release the hold of your past. Forgive those who have hurt you, for holding onto grudges only weighs you down. By forgiving others, you free yourself from the burden of anger and resentment. And remember, forgiveness is not just for them, it is also for yourself. Allow yourself to move forward and let go of the pain.

You are a radiant soul, Claritza. Your beauty shines from within, and it radiates outwards, touching the lives of those around you. Your spirit is infectious, and your positive energy uplifts everyone who crosses your path. Never underestimate the power of your presence.

You are blessed beyond your wildest imagination. Count your blessings every day, no matter how small they may seem. Gratitude is a powerful tool that brings more abundance into your life. Recognize the blessings that surround you, and never take them for granted.

As you continue on your journey, keep living the life of your dreams. You have the power to create the reality you desire. Pursue your passions, follow your heart, and always trust in the process. Your dreams are within reach, and I believe in you wholeheartedly, your future a future filled with love, joy, and fulfillment, may God continue to bless and protect you always.

Keep shining bright, and never stop believing in yourself.

With love and admiration,

Your future self

More About Claritza

Claritza Rausch Peralta is a woman of faith, a devoted mother, and a banking specialist with a passion for writing. Through her inspirational words, she aims to uplift and empower readers, guiding them towards a life filled with purpose, abundance, and love. As a firm believer in the power of positive affirmations, Claritza's devotional books are designed to help readers discover their true identity and potential. In her acclaimed work, "Identified: 31 Days of I Am Affirmations with Bible Verses," she provides a daily dose of encouragement and biblical wisdom, allowing readers to declare their worth and embrace the promises of God.

With a deep understanding that abundance is not just reserved for a select few, Claritza shares her insights in "Believe That Abundance Is Coming." Through powerful stories and practical advice, she inspires readers to shift their mindset, break free from limitations, and open themselves up to the limitless possibilities that await them. Drawing from her own experiences and faith, Claritza's book "Radiant Love" explores the transformative power of love in our lives. With heartfelt anecdotes and spiritual guidance, she encourages readers to cultivate love within themselves and radiate it outwards, spreading joy and positivity to those around them.

In addition to her devotionals, Claritza is dedicated to promoting bilingual education. As a bilingual author, she believes in the importance of language and cultural diversity. Through her books, she seeks to bridge the gap between different communities, fostering understanding and unity. Claritza Rausch Peralta's writing is infused with an inspirational tone that resonates with readers from all walks of life. Her words empower, uplift, and encourage, reminding us of the immense power we hold within ourselves and the divine love that surrounds us.

Through her books, she guides readers on a journey towards self-discovery, abundance, and radiant love.

Claritza Rausch Peralta's work can be purchased on various platforms, including Amazon and her personal website.

Milton Keynes UK
Ingram Content Group UK Ltd.
UKHW042259261123
433027UK00009BC/177/J